Copyright © 2013 Douglas R. Palmer, CPA

All rights reserved.

ISBN-10: 1482676591
ISBN-13: 978-1482676594
Library of Congress Control Number: 2013904399
CreateSpace Independent Publishing Platform, North Charleston, SC

DEDICATION

I would like to dedicate this book to my dear wife, Deborah, and my children, Joseph, William, and Robert, who have supported me through this entire process. I would also like to thank my loving and generous parents, Robert and Bonnie, who provided me with the great gift of education.

CONTENTS

ACKNOWLEDGMENTS

I am deeply thankful to the team of people who helped bring this book together. First, I would like to thank Lori Wark, who helped me with organizing, rewording, streamlining, and completing this project. Next, I am grateful to Fred Foster, who helped guide me through this process, and Greta Palmer for her creative expertise. Finally, I would like to thank Alan Weiss, who gave me the idea for the type of book to create.

PREFACE

I didn't begin my career life advising entrepreneurial companies or starting multiple business. For many years before my first leap into uncharted waters, I only dreamed of the day I would be my own boss and could put all my energy into building my companies.

After years of working for Price Waterhouse (now PwC) auditing and consulting to multinational companies in the 1990s, I was fortunate enough to have the confidence and expertise to start a financial consulting practice in 2002. (We just celebrated our 10-year anniversary last year!)

The dream of starting other entrepreneurial companies and ventures might have remained only a fantasy if a life-threatening event in my 40s hadn't forced me to reflect on what I really wanted to do with the rest of my life.

The old cliché, life is short, suddenly had significant meaning. If I was longing to start other business ventures, I could only ask at this pivotal moment, "What was I waiting for?" In answer to that question, I began making my dream a reality. The past decade hasn't been easy and I came up against some pretty hefty bumps in the road, but I've never looked back.

I've written this handbook for those of you who are dreaming of starting a business, but don't know where to begin or are afraid to move forward as I was. I hope that what I share will help you gather the courage and steer you around the missteps that can occur when starting a new venture.

At the beginning of the handbook, I've listed key points, which are discussed in the following chapter. At the end of each chapter, I list questions to help you understand how the information you've just read should be applied to your particular business. Take time to consider your answers. You may even want to write down your thoughts and ideas. A written record of your learning process is a great roadmap toward making your business more than just an idea.

In chapter three I'll tell you the story of how the title of this book came about, but all you need to know right now is to trust the knowledge you have gained through life experience, follow your passion, turn the page and start walking down that road to your dream. am deeply thankful to the team of people who helped bring this book together.

INTRODUCTION: HOW CHANGING A LIGHT BULB MADE A LIGHT GO OFF

Fortune favors the bold, Fortune favors the brave, Fortune helps the brave, and Fortune favors the strong.
—Latin proverb

THREE KEYS
1. Nothing is guaranteed in life.
2. Life is short.
3. Ask yourself: How do I want to spend this short time on earth?

On a beautiful fall Saturday afternoon in October of 2010, I was working my way through a to-do list of chores. In the process of changing a light bulb, I cut my finger—nothing major, just a slight cut. *Nothing to worry about,* I thought. So I continued to the next item on my list—yard work.

On Monday, the workweek began as usual—meetings with clients—although some pain had developed in my finger. By the end of the day, the throbbing was excruciating. My inclination was to take an Advil and tuck myself into bed, but my wife encouraged me instead to consult with our neighbor across the street who was a doctor.

Upon close examination of the finger and with a furrowed brow, he let me know in no uncertain terms that this small, seemingly insignificant slice in my finger was actually very serious. He urged me to go to the emergency room immediately.

At the hospital that evening, my finger became the center of attention for a group of doctors and nurses. Their concerned faces told me I might not be all right, and no one gave me any assurances that my finger would heal. When my wife started to cry, I knew the inflammation in this cut from a light bulb was not just a simple infection. In fact, I had Methicillin-resistant Staphylococcus aureus staph (MRSA), an infection that can kill. If I were lucky, they said, I would "only" lose a finger or possibly my arm. If unlucky, I would lose my life.

I was immediately admitted as an inpatient, outfitted with a backless blue gown, and hooked up to an IV bag filled with a high dose of antibiotics. Having been given some morphine for my pain, I fell in and out of consciousness while my wife sat by my bedside and the nurses on duty made frequent appearances throughout the night to check my vitals.

For the next three days, I waited for the antibiotics to work their magic. My wife brought our three young sons for short visits, and I tried to reassure them that Daddy would be coming home soon. But the doctors saw little change in the infection and made an executive decision to operate.

I prayed silently that I'd be able to keep my finger, my hand, and ultimately my life. I thought about my kids and wondered if my insurance would cover their next ten-plus years of grade school, high school, and college. I thought about the investments I wished I had made to secure their future, the books that I had hoped to write, and the trip to Spain that my wife and I had wanted to take. I wished that I had been bolder with some of my decisions.

Miraculously, the operation turned out to be a success. And after some further treatment with extreme doses of antibiotics, the MRSA staph infection was gone. Looking back at the original odds given to me by my doctors, I realized that I was, in fact, not only lucky but *extremely* lucky. I also realized that I had been given an opportunity to pursue the hopes that I had considered unfulfilled just twelve hours prior. This was my chance to go for it, to be bolder.

You don't—and shouldn't—need a near-death experience like mine to prompt you to do new things, take new risks, or be bolder. Sometimes, celebrating a milestone birthday, taking a trip, or experiencing a major life change—even a job loss—can inspire motion. But at some point in your life, you need a light bulb moment.

According to insurance actuality tables, when you turn

forty you have forty years left to live. When you're a teenager, forty years seems like an eternity, but after you've checked off a few of life's conventional achievements—high school and college graduation, maybe a postgraduate degree, a wedding, some kids—it's easy to let yourself coast once you hit your midlife mark, instead of maximizing what are arguably your most pivotal years.

To be bold, you need to ask yourself: How do I want to spend the next half of my life? Am I ready to take chances and follow my intuition? Does being bold for me mean starting my own business? If so, this book will help you take your first step.

STEP 1: PLANNING

Plans are nothing; planning is everything.
—Dwight D. Eisenhower

FOUR KEYS

1. Plan for profitability right away, and plan to be profitable quickly.

2. Make sure your revenue is "good," recurring revenue.

3. Do your research before starting your business.

4. Plan the business you desire.

T he big idea…

It goes without saying that having a good idea is the key to a successful business. But what does that really mean? One thing the last decade has taught us with the dot-com boom and bust is that a good idea does not necessarily guarantee business success. So if you've got a big idea, what do you need to do to make it into a successful business? Read on to find out what you need to know to reach your goal and how you can create the kind of company that fits in with the life you want.

Get to Profitability Fast

Throughout my career, I've had the good fortune to work with many different types of businesses, from technology to product to professional-service companies. Over the last ten years, I've served as chief financial officer for several companies. During this time, I've witnessed a lot of companies come and go. As I watch businesses fail and flourish, I've often wondered what made the difference. The answer is: the companies that have staying power are businesses that become profitable quickly. But how do you evaluate whether your big idea can translate into quick profits?

Here are some rules of thumb for profitability:

- You may *not* want to start a business if the expected bottom-line profit after paying yourself a standard market or competitive salary (i.e., what you would pay someone else to do your job) is less than 10 percent of total revenue.

- Your business should have some revenue immediately if you are a service company and at least within a few months if you offer a new product.
- You should strive to be profitable within a year or have the potential to be profitable in that time frame. (A lot of start-up companies could be profitable, but choose to spend more than they earn in order to grow exponentially.)

It may seem obvious, but it still needs to be said that in starting a new business, don't be afraid to make a profit. Many start-ups tend to undercharge as a way to attract clients. If you do, you may find yourself out of business. Remember—if you are not profitable, you will not succeed.

Create Steady, Recurring Revenue

When creating a business, you need to make sure that your business is not only profitable quickly but is also self-sustaining and the revenue is "good" revenue. In other words, you want to have *recurring revenue*. Companies that are only project-based and have sporadic revenue are less likely to succeed. There has to be a recurring element to the revenue so the company can continue to grow its customer base year after year.

If your revenue is project-based, think of ways to create recurring revenue. Project-based revenue can be very lucrative. Some companies survive solely on project revenue for extended periods of time. However, these companies suffer during economic downturns.

If you follow companies that are publicly traded, you will notice that Wall Street also values recurring-revenue businesses more highly. The stock of project-based companies tends to trade lower because of the unpredictable viability of that business model.

Find Your Business Model

It makes more sense to start a business based on a business model that is proven. So, when you're planning your company, look for similar businesses and investigate the models they are using. Why reinvent the wheel if there are examples to copy? If you are thinking about starting a company with a business model that is unproven, make sure you invest your time researching your chosen industry before you do.

Here are some methods for gathering the critical information you need before deciding on a business model.

Search the Internet

Before you start your business, doing a quick Internet search will provide you a list of companies that are similar to the business you want to create. For example, when I started my restaurant-feedback business, I did extensive research on the restaurant industry through the Internet. Since I was also interested in creating an app, I searched to find out what apps were already available and which niche hadn't been filled yet.

Cold-Call Business Owners

You can do a lot of research by simply calling the

owners of other companies. Although these owners could be considered competitors, most are very happy to talk about their businesses to help those just starting out.

Use Focus Groups

If you're starting a company with a business model that is unproven, try interviewing a random group of people to get their opinions about your business idea. Don't be shy about discussing your idea because of the fear your plan could be stolen. The chances of someone starting a business after hearing your idea is highly unlikely, and in general, people are honest and want to help.

In my opinion, when starting a business, you should tell as many people as possible as a way to gather ideas; even one good idea gleaned from someone you respect can help your business dramatically. In addition, the people you tell may also have connections to others willing to lend a hand toward your success.

(Although I do advocate spreading the word about your "big idea," I remind you it is important to use your best judgment when considering taking someone into your confidence. Make sure your confidantes are trustworthy and have your best interests at heart. Also, confiding in too many people may be detrimental in some circumstances.)

Be Your Own Customer

Use your own product or service! Make sure you, your family, and your friends try out, test, and discover the benefits of your company's product. If you or the people whose opinions you trust do not love and use the product or service, chances are pretty good that others will not be enchanted with what you are trying to sell either.

Find a Mentor

Mentors are worth their weight in gold. There's always someone who is more seasoned than you are. So if you are starting a business, you'll want to find a mentor. Your mentor should be trustworthy and able to give you advice, lend support, or just be a great partner for brainstorming ideas. This person is different from the rest of the people in whom you confide. A mentor is someone who has been, or still is, in a similar business. Here are some ideas on where and how to find a mentor.

- Virtual mentorship

Thanks to social networking, it's much easier these days to find people in your field and beyond. If you have a sense of whom you would like to connect with, consider asking for an informational interview. After your relationship is established, set up regular check-ins through in-person meetings, on the phone, or through Skype. If you are looking to expand your network and learn about new people, start by exploring blogs on topics that pertain to your business. Follow the authors on social media, and engage with them by asking questions and sharing useful information.

- Mentoring opportunities at professional organizations[1]

If you think a more formal mentoring program would

---

[1] Idealist Careers.

work better for you, many professional organizations offer mentoring programs and opportunities. Here is a list of ways to use professional associations to help you get started.

1. Contact your university career office or alumni association.

Contact your alumni association and see if they hold networking events or facilitate connections with mentors. A mentor who went to the same school as you is a natural fit. For example, I really enjoyed the "Mentor for a Morning" program I attended at Baruch College's School of Public Affairs. I got to sit down for twenty minutes with three arts and cultural executives and discuss my career goals. It was kind of like speed dating for mentors!

2. Identify a mentor across sectors.

Are there people you admire because of the career choices they have made, even if they don't work in your field or sector? Career decisions and advice are highly transferable across industries. If you are already connected to this person, schedule a meeting and discuss why you feel inspired by their work.

3. Set up your own peer-mentoring program.

Are there smart, motivated colleagues whom you look up to? As opposed to mentoring up, consider mentoring across. Get together with a small, defined group of people on a regular basis to discuss strategies, career goals, and new projects. You'll never know what experiences and insights your colleagues possess unless you ask.

Focus on Passion

Over the last decade, the trend for start-up businesses has been to work around the clock to create a successful business with the sole purpose of being bought by another company down the road. This "business model" can certainly be one way to "get rich quick," but what if that hoped-for big sale never happens? If you're not passionate about the company you're building for its own sake, if the enjoyment of creating something from scratch and seeing it flourish is not enough, or if your pride in what you are creating isn't part of the equation, you may be in for a huge letdown and find yourself left with a company you care nothing about if that dream buyer never materializes. Passion is what keeps you going through the inevitable highs and lows of building a business.

Create a Lifestyle Business

Before you even think about putting a shingle out announcing your business, reflect on what you want your personal life to be. Starting and running a business is time-consuming and can grab every free moment you once treasured. If you want time for yourself, your family, or special activities you just can't give up, you need to create a "lifestyle" business.

Here are some ideas on how to create a business that allows for a life outside of work:

- Create a business that you can manage from anywhere by putting systems in place that keep everything virtual:
  - Go paperless by scanning everything and storing it

in the cloud.
- Consider using a service like Dropbox or Google Docs for your file storage.
- Use an application like Evernote to store and organize pdf files.
- Look into a VOIP (voice over Internet Protocol) system, such as Vonage, so you can receive phone calls wherever you are.
- Use employees to scale your business, but keep them virtual. (You do not want to be required to go into "the office" just because you have employees working in a particular building.)
- If you are a service business, create a revenue model that charges customers monthly regardless of hours worked.
- If you are selling a product, create virtual fulfillment in all areas including customer support.

You are starting down this road because it's your passion. The joy you have for your business will be tested if you don't allow for personal time. In fact, getting away from the business for short periods and allowing for reflection, will bring more clarity on ways to make your passion a success.

Handbook Questions:

- Is my revenue recurring? How can I adjust the model so that I will have recurring revenue?
- Have I thoroughly researched my business? Have I found a mentor for this business?
- Do I want a lifestyle business? How can I arrange my business so that I will have a lifestyle business?

STEP 2: PLAN FOR GROWTH AND SCALE

Give me a lever long enough and a fulcrum on which to place it, and I shall move the world.
—Archimedes

THREE KEYS
1. Plan for scale, and scale quickly!
2. Delegate 80 percent of everything you do.
3. Create a five-year plan; create a one-year plan.

Immediately after starting your business, begin focusing your efforts on preparing for growth. You do not want to be caught off guard when your company begins to generate substantial revenue.

Scalability: Plan for Growth

When planning your business, remember to build a business that has "scalability," meaning your business has the ability to grow exponentially without becoming overwhelmed or inefficient. Scalability also describes a business that can essentially manage itself after a period of time or one that someone can step in and run without downtime.

A service business where one person performs the service will never be a scalable business. Although this type of company might be a business for some people, it's not a business that will grow exponentially and take off. So, when you're planning your business, make sure you plan for scalability if your intention is to grow.

Scalability requires the delegation of tasks. Steven Covey, author of *The 7 Habits of Highly Effective People*, uses the Pareto Principle to explain why delegation is so critical. The Pareto Principle states that 80 percent of outcomes result from 20 percent of the focus. In other words, if you have one hundred things slated on your to-do list, only twenty are really important. Therefore, out of all the things done during the day, only 20 percent really matter. When considering revenue, the same rules apply. Twenty percent of your effort produce 80 percent of your revenue. Any more time spent is really wasted. As a business owner, you should, therefore, be spending your time on the important 20 percent and delegating the remaining 80 percent.

Here are some steps for creating scalability quickly without increasing the company cost dramatically:

- Hire virtual employees.
- Use time zones to your advantage. In today's world, you can hire good employees just about anywhere in the world, which enables your business to produce products or serve clients around the clock.
- Partner with a larger company to deliver your product or service through different channels.
- Use an outsourced sales force to sell your product or service.
- Keep everything in the cloud, and use cloud-based services such as Dropbox, Evernote, and QuickBooks Online.

Craft Your Five-Year Plan

Writing down a five-year plan is essential. The act of creating a plan that looks into the future will force you to focus on the goals of your company and lays out exactly how you plan to reach those goals.

In creating a five-year plan, keep in mind several key points:

- Costs: be realistic.

It's very tempting to lowball or ignore expenses when drawing up a five-year plan. Frequently, key cost items are overlooked or forgotten; the business owner's salary, infrastructure costs, and technology needs may be forgotten or the figures be estimated too low. If you have a cyclical business, take those cycles into account as well.

- Revenue: be realistic.

Revenue projections should also be accurate and tied to specific metrics or something tangible. I've seen instances where revenue projections are in reality wishful thinking. Although looking at the "good" numbers may make you feel better, it's not helping you build a successful company.

Analyze Your Five-Year Plan

After you have completed your financial projections, take a high-level view of what you've created. Don't get wrapped up in the specifics of how to create an Excel spreadsheet. Instead, take a long, hard look at the numbers. If the projections are not achievable and seem out of reach, you need to rethink your plan.

Plan for Headaches

I met someone a while back who had just started his own business. Prior to setting up a windshield-replacement company, he had worked, for over two decades, in sales for the car parts industry. Although he had previously sold replacement windshields to companies while working at his former job, he had never owned a business. Starting a business specializing in a particular car part replacement— windshields—sounded like a good opportunity and an easy transition from employee to employer. Unfortunately, having only worked for a large company, he didn't take into account the problems and issues he would now have to face as an owner. The aggravation was so extreme that his new company deeply affected his personal, family, and financial life. The moral of this story is make sure you understand the headaches involved with the business you are starting.

Handbook Questions:

- How can I immediately create scale to my business?
- Do I have a five-year plan? Do I have a one-year plan?
- Are my revenue and cost figures realistic?
- Have I considered outsourcing all aspects of my business?

Am I delegating all of my noncore activities? Am I delegating 80 percent of all activities?

STEP 3: EXECUTION

To be your own man is a hard business. If you try it, you will be lonely often, and sometimes frightened. But no price is too high to pay for the privilege of owning yourself.
—Rudyard Kipling

THREE KEYS
1. Form a legal entity right away.
2. Build your virtual team of advisors right away.
3. Build your brand and web presence right away.

T rust your legs.

When I started my company over ten years ago, I had been in the working world for about a decade and I thought I knew all there was to know about accounting, finance, and serving customers. Even so, I was a bit nervous at the prospect of starting my own company. Then someone gave me a piece of advice that I'll always remember: "Trust your legs." Those three words made a lot of sense to me. If I work very hard eight hours a day and trust myself, I won't fail. The key to starting a business is just to do it! If you have enough expertise, the willingness to start a business, and the ability to trust yourself, trust your legs. That's not to say that every business you start will be a home run. You may have some failures along the way, but you'll learn from each of your attempts. The worst thing that can happen is you get a job working for someone else down the road because your business failed. Perhaps, this will only be a temporary working arrangement until you start your new company with the knowledge gained from experience.

Form a Company

Your "big idea" becomes a real business when you legally form a company. A lot of people start serving customers and transacting business without forming a legal structure. Taking this official step, however, will start you thinking and acting more like a business. So, what type of legal structure should you form?

- Limited Liability Company

If you plan to run a business as a one-person sole proprietorship, you may want to consider forming a single-member limited liability company (LLC). An LLC is a flexible enterprise that blends elements of partnership and corporate structures and provides limited liability to its owners. In other words, if the company is sued, only the assets in the company are at risk. Your personal assets, such as housing and personal investments, remain off limits to any legal action. Record keeping is also simpler than other forms of legal entities, as annual meetings and minutes are not required. Owners report their earnings from the business on their personal tax returns (called pass-through taxation) thus avoiding double taxation.

- Partnership Limited Liability Company

If you plan on having a partner, a partnership limited liability company provides the same liability protection as the LLC. The partners report their earnings from the business on their personal tax returns, thus avoiding double taxation.

- Corporation

If you're planning a company that will have shareholders and possibly some private equity and you have a goal of ultimately going public, you may want to consider forming a corporation. Corporations allow multiple shares of equity classes and flexibility for certain equity transactions. As with an LLC, your personal assets are protected.

- S Corporation

Another type of legal entity to consider is the S corporation. In general, S corporations (or S corps) are corporations that elect to pass corporate income, losses, deductions, and credit through to their shareholders for federal tax purposes. Shareholders of S corporations report the income and losses on their personal tax returns and are assessed tax at their individual income tax rates. This allows S corporations to avoid double taxation on the corporate income.

If the thought of creating a legal entity is overwhelming, take heart. The process is actually pretty simple. A company can be created in a matter of hours. It usually only requires filling out a form and creating articles of organization. To find the form and a how-to on creating the articles of organization, go to your state's government website and look for examples of suggested articles. Type your own articles up, and send them to the state. Once the company is registered, you can apply for a federal tax ID. Getting a federal tax ID takes less than fifteen minutes and can be completed online. With that done, you're off to the races.

Bring Your Brand to Life

From light bulbs to cars to fish sticks brands are all around us. To break through the clutter a business must create brand recognition --one your customer base will come to know and recognize at a glance. Many elements established a company's branding, but the following are two ways to begin the process of making your mark.

- Get a logo.

A logo is how people will identify your business and is the core to branding your company. The logo doesn't have to be complicated. There are a number of companies and independent designers who can create your logo. Some companies send out jobs to designers for bid (e.g., www.99designs.com). They don't charge a lot, and the bidding process allows you to select from a variety of designers. The way this works is you submit your requirements for your logo, and then designers around the country—and sometimes around the world—start submitting their designs for your selection. The designer who created the logo you want to use is the one who gets paid.

- Create a website.

A website is the face of your business, so it's important to get the look that's right for your company. Before you can begin thinking about the design of your site, you'll need to register a domain name. A domain name is the URL or address of your website. It should be easy to remember and include the name of your company.

Creating websites can be very simple these days. Online one-stop shops will help you with all the pieces you need. With a standard website package, you can order the domain name, establish a place to host your site, set up email addresses, and create a website. Yahoo Small Business and Google both have full-service solutions that make this job relatively easy. This is all done through a website, so if you have questions or are confused, getting a live person to speak to could be a challenge.

If you will be selling products through your website, you may also be able to create a "store" through this one-stop shop. If not, sites such as Yahoo and Google have merchant accounts for credit-card processing. Setting up a PayPal account is another way to facilitate transactions.

Be aware that creating a website through these services does require some technological knowledge. Also, since these companies use templates, you run the risk of having a website that looks like a thousand other websites.

If you want a distinctive look, seek out a company or designer specializing in web design, user-interface theory, web infrastructure, navigation, coding, and search-engine optimization so your site can be found on the Internet. Many of these specialized companies can also help you with domain registration and hosting, as well as maintaining your site once it's live.

Gather your support team.

Any good manger knows that he or she is only as good as his or her support team. Creating a group of people with specialized skills makes running a business easier and makes you look good. Here are some key team players to consider.

- Banker

It's very important to create a good banking relationship. A banker who understands small businesses and is willing to work closely with you can help set up accounts appropriate for your business, establish a line of credit to cover large outlays or working capital needs, and resolve problems. Having a relationship with someone at the bank alleviates many of the headaches in managing the finances of a small business.

- CPA /Accountant

As you begin to set up systems and processes, I would highly recommend engaging with an accountant. The accountant can set up your books for the business in accounting software and can also train you on how to use the software. At the end of each year, the accountant will check your work and create your tax return.

Some businesses may need to submit quarterly payments for such items as unemployment insurance, estimated taxes, and property taxes. Your accountant will remind you when these taxes are due and can file for you—one less thing for you to worry about.

I also recommend hiring a bookkeeper or a staff accountant to maintain your accounting records and prepare financial reports. Having an accounting team on board will take these tasks off your plate so you can focus on growing your business.

- Lawyer

A good lawyer will not only make sure your company structure is sound and in accordance with your business needs but will also help in the writing of various agreements so you can expedite transactions. What type of agreements? For starters, when you begin hiring employees, you're going to need a good employment agreement. When you deal with customers, an engagement agreement is necessary. If you have proprietary software or products that you want to tell people about but don't want the information disclosed, you will need a nondisclosure agreement.

Handbook Questions:

- Have you formed a legal entity?
- Have you engaged the services of a CPA or a lawyer?
- Do you have a relationship with a banker?

STEP 4: FIND FUNDING

Do all you can to make your dreams come true.
—Joel Osteen

FIVE KEYS

1. Look into obtaining a small business loan through the Small Business Administration (SBA).

2. Raise angel funding from friends and family first.

3. Attend angel meetings before presenting to potential investors.

4. Make sure you have investor documents ready to go.

5. Confirm your near-term revenue targets are achievable and the next quarter is almost a given.

Having solid financial and legal partners as part of your team from the beginning is particularly important if you are raising money and dealing with investors. You want those interested in your company to feel confident that your business is structured properly and financially sound. Once your financial advisers are in place, here are some suggestions for where to look for funding.

- Small Business Administration Loans

Now may be a great time to raise money via debt (instead of equity). Here are five reasons why:

1. Low Interest Rate—With interest rates so low right now, debt is cheap. A few Small Business Administration (SBA) deals appear to be priced inexpensively relative to an equity finance cost of capital. This means that opportunities may exist to benefit greatly from the gains due to leverage.

2. Tax Benefit—Interest on debt is tax deductible, whereas dividends on equity are not (and actually may be taxable). In fact, the higher the marginal tax rate of the company, the higher the amount of debt a company should have in its tax structure.

3. Discipline to Owners/Management—Debt adds an element of discipline to an organization. The old adage "Equity is a cushion; debt is a sword" certainly applies. In fact, the management teams of firms with high cash flows left over each year are more likely to be complacent and inefficient.

4. Continuity of Ownership—Financing through debt keeps the control of an organization intact.

5. Creditor Disinterest in Owning Your Business— One of the biggest downsides to debt is the

possibility of being forced into bankruptcy and/or being taken over by a lending institution. Although this is possible, banks typically have no interest in taking over a company that has fallen behind in interest payments (or broken a financial agreement). Banks would much rather work with a company than take it over.

- Family, Friends, and Angel Investors

Before your company goes for a big round of funding, the first place to start is your friends and family. However, if the company does not do well, problems could arise and jeopardize close relationships. The second option is to look for angel investors. Angel investors are usually investors in the community who want to help local entrepreneurs. Angels fund between $100,000 to $500,000 as seed money. They are frequently business owners themselves who were helped along the way. Although angel investors want to make a profit on their investment in a start-up company, they tend to be motivated more by lending a helping hand and being a mentor to entrepreneurs.

In most major markets, there are a number of angel groups. Here is a short list:

- New York Angels Inc., New York City
- Dingman Angels, Washington DC and Maryland
- Golden Seeds LLC, New York City
- Investors' Circle, San Francisco, California
- Tech Coast Angels, Los Angeles, California
- Ohio TechAngel Funds, Columbus, Ohio
- North Coast Angel Fund, Cleveland, Ohio
- Band of Angels, Menlo Park, California

- Hyde Park Angel Network, Chicago
- Alliance of Angels, Seattle, Washington
- Pasadena Angels, Altadena, California

To find angel investment groups near you, I suggest searching the Internet and contacting the business school at your local university. If these avenues do not work, ask your accountant or lawyer; he or she is bound to have a connection to an angel group.

- Venture Capitalists

Venture capitalists fund companies in larger amounts than angel investors. They also tend to invest money in stages, called series. The influx of dollars is based upon the developmental stage of the business and the potential for the return on investment.

What Investors Want to Know

Investors interested in investing in a company look very closely at the prospective business. To evaluate whether or not a business is a good choice, potential investors will ask for several documents so they can predict the likelihood of success or failure.

Five-Year Plan

Remember that five-year plan you created when first outlining your big idea? Take a look at this document and update as needed. Investors will want to review your plan to make sure you have thought through how you will reach your company goals.

One-Year Projection

Unlike the five-year plan, the one-year projection should include more specifics and actual costs and revenue figures. For example, your five-year plan may have revenue and costs based upon assumptions driven on a metric of expected headcount. Your one-year plan, in contrast, should have real costs (e.g., actual employees working today and throughout the year, actual rent costs now, actual revenue now, and expected revenue based on a sales pipeline). In addition, make sure the projected revenue and expenses in the upcoming quarter will be met. For example, if you have sales to just one customer so far, a projected revenue for the next month with expected sales to twenty customers is not realistic.

One Pager

After you have created well-thought-out one-year and five-year projections, focus on getting together a one pager, a document that summarizes your business and has three- to five-year financial projections and a summary. A one pager is essentially a snapshot of the business. When an investor reads this concise write-up, he or she should know why your company is a great investment. In many cases, investors don't even want to look at the financial projections, but they do want to see the one pager. As with everyone these days, the investor's time is limited, so he or she needs to be able to understand your business at a glance. Since this is your best shot at getting an investor intrigued enough to take the next step, put in the time and effort to make this document stand out.

The Private Placement Memorandum

After you have your one pager, the next step is to work with a good law firm to draw up a private placement memorandum (PPM).

A PPM is created to fund a business by selling securities, which are sold through a private offering, mostly to a small number of accredited investors with a net worth of over one million or an annual income of over two hundred thousand per year.

This document in some respects is much more than one would need to raise angel funds; however, if you're going after a large round of funding and you want to be in accordance with rules and regulations, then you need a private placement memorandum. Some law firms charge top dollar for this work, so I would recommend placing a cap on legal fees.

You've Got Funding. Now What?

At the beginning of this handbook, I noted that not getting to profitability quickly is one of the biggest mistakes I see made by start-up business. It's all too common for businesses to fail because a company never becomes self-sustaining. The same is true even if you've been fortunate in finding investors.

If a company relies on continual investor funding rounds to pay for its costs, eventually, investors are going to pull out. Therefore, your company must become profitable quickly regardless of your luck in finding investors.

Handbook Questions:

- Have I looked into an SBA loan? Is my business suitable for an SBA loan? Have I asked my banker on my team about an SBA loan?
- Have I approached friends and family about my business funding first?
- Have I attended an angel meeting? Have I asked my accountant and lawyer about a good angel group?
- Do I have a one pager? Do I have one-year projections? Do I have five-year projections?
- Is my information in the one-year projection achievable? Is the information in the five-year projections realistic?

STEP 5: THE PITCH

Most of the important things in the world have been accomplished by people who have kept on trying when there seemed to be no hope at all.
—Dale Carnegie

THREE KEYS
1. Get lots of help when hiring your sales team.
2. The sales team is the most critical hire.
3. Become your company's best salesperson.

H<small>ire a sales and marketing team.</small>

A creative, talented, and assertive sales team is critical to any business. In fact, the best salespeople frequently get paid more than the founders of the company because the sales staff brings in customers and grows the revenue.

I would recommend getting help in hiring the sales staff, whether through a recruiting agency or an experienced human resource professional. Remember, if you hire the wrong person for the job, you may not feel the effects of this bad decision for many months.

I would also recommend requiring prospective employees to take a series of tests. Look for companies that help businesses hire people using aptitude tests specifically geared to evaluating those looking for jobs in sales. A good company to hire for employee measurement tools and screening tests is a company located outside of Pittsburgh called PSP METRICS.[2]

Don't pass up the opportunity to check references to make sure the candidates were really as successful at their former jobs as their résumé makes you believe.

Accountability

Make salespeople accountable.

My number-one rule of growing a sales team is to develop a plan that outlines your expectations for your

---

[2] http://www.pspmetrics.com/.

sales force.

Sales people are notorious for "hitting" their numbers early in the quarter and then coasting for the rest of the quarter, backdating or forward dating to disguise their tactics. Therefore, management should set up systems of daily accountability for the people who sell the company's products.

Remote Salespeople

If your salespeople are virtual or located at a remote location, make sure their pay structure is as close to 100 percent commission as possible. Or move a founding partner or employee to the new location. I have seen time after time the same scenario: A company wants to open a remote office in Chicago, for example. The CEO then hires a person living in Chicago to grow the business. What happens? The salesperson usually lives off the large base salary for a few months and assembles a "pipeline" that never seems to convert to customers. The salesperson then moves on to a different job. Watch out.

Sell Yourself

In addition to hiring salespeople to dramatically grow your company and revenue, you must also sell yourself. You may not be a good salesperson, or maybe you just think you're not a good salesperson, but you should at least make an effort to sell whenever the opportunity arises. This means you need an elevator speech ready to go. An elevator speech is a brief statement describing your company. The message should be short enough to be delivered in the amount of time it takes to ride an elevator from one floor to another.

Here are tips for creating your own elevator speech with the 5Q Process™[3]:

- Figure out what keeps your target market up at night. What frustrates them? Scares them? Fills them with greed?
- Find that one thing you do that *none* of your competitors do to address that problem.
- Be specific about how you would address the problem.
- Make sure your pitch is brief and easy to remember. Keep it to twenty seconds or less.
- Try your new statement out on colleagues and prospects.
- If you get a good response to your elevator speech and you feel comfortable with its message, use it as your tagline and in all marketing.

Here is the standard elevator speech for our financial outsourcing business:

"I am a partner in a boutique financial service company located in Bethesda, Maryland. We serve as the finance department for many growing organizations. Many companies truly need strong financial oversight and reporting but cannot afford to hire a full-time CFO. We have a staff of senior financial executives and CPAs who serve our clients by handling not only CFO-related matters but also all accounting matters. We are different from other 'Virtual CFO' companies because we handle all aspects of

---

[3] Producer's eSource.

company finance and accounting—not just the highest level."

If you really feel strongly that you're not skilled at selling, hire a sales consultant to teach you how to sell your own company.

Handbook Questions:

- Have you hired a sales team, or are you the only one trying to sell for your business?
- Have you engaged a recruiting firm to help you build your sales team?
- Do you screen your sales personnel with personality and intelligence tests? Do you perform background checks?
- Are your salespeople remote? If so, how are they compensated? How are they held accountable?

STEP 6: PREPARE FOR GROWTH

You were born to win, but to be a winner, you must plan to win, prepare to win, and expect to win.
—Zig Ziglar

THREE KEYS
1. Create systems for all areas of your business.
2. Build your business to scale.
3. Think BIG.

True story, a few years ago, I found myself consulting with two very similar professional-service organizations. Let's call one "Company A" and the other "Company B." Company A's business strategy was to outsource all aspects of its noncore business, add partners for each revenue line item, and open offices with core employees.

Company B was similar but did the following: outsourced most core functions; did *not* include new partners or offer equity to any of its employees; and tried to open offices with unknown noncore virtual employees. What happened?

Company A grew its revenue exponentially and eventually sold the business to a larger company. Company B grew slightly but is still about the same size as it was five years ago. Moral of the story: consider adding partners (or more key employees) if you want to grow.

Issuing Equity

While it is important for businesses to "guard" company equity at times, it is also important that prospective investors and employees be rewarded with equity. Here are a few times:

- Angel/initial round raises—Many entrepreneurs get so focused on company valuations (when there is not even a proven business model) that they lose out on investment capital due to these valuations being too high. In addition, entrepreneurs sometimes turn away investors because they think that they have raised enough capital and they do not want to dilute the company shares.

- Employee rewards—Many company founders are stingy with stock options for employees. Again, they feel that they do not want to "dilute" the company value with option shares. What entrepreneurs fail to realize is that stock options tend to keep the employees dedicated. And dedicated employees are usually the sole reason for a company's success (or failure). I can think of numerous examples of companies that did not include employees in option rounds and ultimately failed.

I still maintain that companies need to guard equity in situations where a company is strong and profitable. However, for companies that are just starting out, founders may want to share the wealth—because 100 percent of zero is...zero!

Create Systems

Immediately after creating your business, focus on creating systems. If you set up a business and just do everything yourself, that's not truly a business; it's just you working for yourself. At some point, a business needs to be able to run itself and still generate income. A company also needs to be designed so anyone can step in and possibly buy the company without downtime. To reach these goals, you need to create solid, efficient systems.

- **Accounting**

Set up an accounting and billing system so that anyone

can step in and do the accounting for your business.

• Bookkeeping

Create a separate bank account for your business. Any business expenses should be paid with a business check or credit card specifically identified for your business. It doesn't matter if the credit card is in the company name or your personal name; that card should be just for your business.

You will want to begin tracking your expenses and your revenue in accounting software almost immediately. Companies just starting out should probably begin with QuickBooks. A lot of people think that QuickBooks is a software package for very small organizations; however, I've seen large companies use it. The software is intuitive and simple to use. QuickBooks is also inexpensive relative to other accounting software. You can get a QuickBooks license for under two hundred dollars. Once the software is purchased, download and install it on your computer. Most accountants also use QuickBooks, so sharing your account records with your accountant will be easy and efficient.

QuickBooks has introduced a web-based product. By signing up on their website, you have access to the software without downloading it to your computer. The advantage to this method is that you can manage your account anywhere you have access to the Internet. There is a monthly fee for this service, which is based on the level of functionality you require.

• Sales

Lay out a process that specifies how sales are done, what happens after the sale is finalized, and the paperwork needed for the sale.

Also, consider using sales software, such as Salesforce.com. Salesforce.com offers all of the sales software tools that you need to grow your company. The application is cloud-based with no software or hardware to install. Once an account is set up, you should see a positive impact on your business right away.

Creating a process is not only good for the smooth operation of your company; it's also good for your peace of mind. When a system is in place, there's no need to wonder what needs to be done next.

Handbook Questions:

- Do you have a good software system for your accounting?
- Are you trying to grow your business? Have you considered adding a partner? Have you considered combining your firm with another similar company or becoming a partner in another firm?
- Have you issued equity to key personnel or investors?
- Do you currently use good sales software?

STEP 7: STICK WITH IT

Advantage comes not from the spectacular or the technical. Advantage comes from a persistent seeking of the mundane edge.
—Tom Peters

THREE KEYS
1. Keep the momentum going.
2. Don't let perfection get in the way.
3. Reward yourself.

M omentum…

As noted by J. B. Glossinger of morningcoach.com, when people make a resolution or set out on a program of improvement, motivation and commitment usually find their way to the dumpster in about ninety days. The same can be said for starting a business. The first ninety days of a new company are filled with excitement and lots of anticipation for growth. After this period, the momentum starts to dissipate. Thoughts like *Why did I get started in this?* or *This is not as much fun as I anticipated* start to make an appearance.

The key to overcoming a slump in motivation is awareness and focus.

Here are some tips from the morningcoach.com blog:

- If the business seems overwhelming, take one step at a time. (As the old saying goes: How do you eat an elephant? One bite at a time.)
- Treat each day as if it were the first day of your business.
- Education creates momentum and inspiration, so go to classes, join workshops, and watch instructional videos.
- Don't forget to reward yourself with each new win: "Ring the bell!"

Perfection

Perfection is not always what it's cracked up to be.

For business owners, moving forward and creating new opportunities is the key to progress. Companies need to continually put something out there. In the words of inspirational trainer and speaker Fred Foster, "It is more important to be accurate than to be precise." For example, if you are shooting at a target, it is better to have more shots in the circle around the bull's-eye than to actually hit the bull's-eye.

This means that even if a project is only 80 percent or 90 percent perfect, it is better to move forward than to strive for 100 percent perfection because while you're trying to be perfect, you may miss an opportunity.

Our firm recently used this approach when our tax app for the Android and iPhone was created. We could have spent another month redesigning the interface or including more tax data but decided to finalize and launch the app before the end of the tax year. This worked well, and we have had thousands of downloads.

It is important to create and build continually. When doing so, be sure not to let perfection get in the way of action.

Handbook Questions:

- How do I keep the momentum going after starting my business?
- Is my energy level high? Am I "ringing the bell" with each new win?
- Am I a perfectionist? Is this getting in the way of action?

STEP 8: PLAN FOR SUCCESS

By failing to prepare, you are preparing to fail.
—Benjamin Franklin

FOUR KEYS
1. Have a strategic plan.
2. Regularly update and refer back to your plan.
3. Make sure you have a big enough *why*.
4. Invite in success; imagine success; be successful.

T he strategic plan…

I've spent a lot of time in this book discussing ways to plan your business. Most of the planning included Excel spreadsheets, number crunching, and research. To develop a strategic plan, throw away the Excel, forget the numbers, and close down the Internet. This is the time for you to have fun and imagine the company of your dreams.

The strategic plan is composed of the following short statements:

Vision Statement
In a paragraph of twenty to thirty words, describe the kind of business you want to create. Consider such factors as:

- How big or small do you want your company to be?
- Who are your ideal clients?
- What services or products will you provide?
- How will your business fit with the lifestyle you want?

Mission Statement
With this twenty- to thirty-word statement, you get to tell *why* you are pursing your vision. What's your reason for starting this particular business, and what special talents or experiences do you possess that will make your vision a reality?

Scope
When starting a business, it's tempting to assume you

can meet any need of any client. This isn't realistic or particularly productive. You need to establish boundaries. If the scope of your business is too narrow, the probability for success may be diminished because of fewer potential customers. If the scope is too broad, you may be pulled in too many directions and never have the time to focus on what is important. (Don't forget about the 20/80 rule!)

Assumptions

Writing down your assumptions in regard to your business is important because what you assume can determine how your business will grow and prosper. The more specific these assumptions, the better.

Here are a few examples:

- I will keep my present job for the next twelve months.
- There is a lot of competition in my chosen field, but few companies provide the customer service I plan to deliver.
- I will limit my involvement to twenty hours per week for the first twelve months.
- I have ten customers that I can start with right now.

Goals and Objectives

If you don't know where you're headed, how will you know when you get there? The list of your goals and objectives is your road map to a successful company. This list should be specific, measurable, and attainable within one to three years. Some examples follow:

- Be able to quit my present job within twelve months.

- Grow the business to generate $100,000 gross sales in the first year of operation.
- Add fifty new customers by the end of the first year of business.

Risk

It's important to list as many risks as you can identify. Knowing the risks will help you prepare ahead of time in case you hit a bump in the road:

Following are some possible risks:

- Loss of customers due to competition.
- Major technical meltdown.
- Loss of lease, requiring a new location and facility be found.

Strategies

Your strategies are the methods you will use to achieve your goals and objectives in spite of the risks.

Here are some examples:

- Hold monthly free workshops (generates loyal customers).
- Publish a monthly newsletter (excellent marketing).
- Develop backup computer systems.
- Create an employee benefits package that attracts and keeps great employees on board.

Progress Reporting

Now that you've got your strategic plan in place, don't let it just sit there. Your company is constantly changing, and your plan needs to reflect those changes. Review your plan at least monthly and update as needed. The strategic plan is also a great way to track your progress. Unfortunately, sometimes the plan will not have good news. If you find the goals you set are elusive, you may need to reevaluate them or admit failure. There's no shame in failing. Pulling up stakes may be the smart thing to do to avoid major financial losses.

If this go-round at a business didn't work out, perform a postmortem. Take a hard look at the plan, and find out what went wrong. Ask yourself if there was anything you could have done before it was too late? This type of in-depth analysis will make you better prepared and wiser when starting your next business.

Handbook Questions:

- Do you have a business and strategic plan?
- Do you regularly refer back to and update your plan?
- Do you have a BIG why for your plan?

CONCLUSION

Risk is going to Afghanistan and getting your head blown off.
—Howard Stern

.

I was listening to Howard Stern, a famous radio DJ, one morning on my way to work. He was discussing an actor who was up for an Academy Award. The actor said something to the effect that he was now happy that he had agreed to take on such a risky role. Howard then so eloquently pointed out that that is *not risk*. "Risk is going to Afghanistan and getting your head blown off," he said.

Howard Stern may not have defined risk in the most gracious manner, but the point is clear. There are risks, and then there are *risks*. Starting your own business is not easy, and there's no guarantee of success, but is it a risk to try? (As my opening story in this book shows, starting a business may be less risky than changing a light bulb.)

Although putting your dreams on the back burner may seem safe, perhaps the greater risk is to regret never having taken the chance. So be aware, do your homework, take a deep breath, gather your passion, internalize your vision, get started and **trust your legs**!

ABOUT THE AUTHOR

Douglas Palmer is an accomplished entrepreneur and business advisor. For over two decades, he has been a CPA and CFO serving large and small organizations both domestically and abroad. He has personally started multiple companies and now advises business owners. His firm has been in business for over a decade and currently sponsors the University of Maryland entrepreneurial program. Doug also works with UMD students on a pro-bono basis.

Doug serves on numerous boards and is the chairman of St. John's Community Services Foundation, one of the oldest charities in Washington DC.

Doug, his wife, Deborah, and their three children live in Maryland just outside of Washington DC.

www.ingramcontent.com/pod-product-compliance
Lightning Source LLC
Chambersburg PA
CBHW051242170526
45165CB00004B/1539